The New

ANALYZING
FINAN
STATE
25 KEYS TO THE NUM

ERIC PRESS, PH.D., CPA
Fox School of Business and Management
Temple University

Lebhar-Friedman Books
NEW YORK • CHICAGO • LOS ANGELES • LONDON • PARIS • TOKYO

For *The New York Times*
Mike Levitas, Editorial Director, Book Development
Tom Redburn, General Series Editor
Brent Bowers, Series Editor
James Schembari, Series Editor

Lebhar-Friedman Books
425 Park Avenue
New York, NY 10022

Published by Lebhar-Friedman Books
Lebhar-Friedman Books is a company of Lebhar-Friedman Inc.

Printed in the United States of America

Library of Congress Cataloging-in-Publication Data
Press, Eric.
    Analyzing financial statements : 25 keys to understanding the
numbers / Eric Press.
    p. cm.—(The New York Times pocket MBA series ; v. 1)
Includes index.
ISBN 0-86730-771-4 (pbk.)
1. Financial statements.   I. Title.   II. Series.
HF5681.B2P734   1999
657'.3—dc21   99-37749
                                                          CIP

DESIGN & PRODUCTION BY MILLER WILLIAMS DESIGN ASSOCIATES

Visit our Web site at lfbooks.com

LEBHAR-FRIEDMAN BOOKS is proud to present *The New York Times* Pocket MBA Series, 12 invaluable reference volumes that are easily accessible to all businesspersons, from first level managers to the executive suite. The books are written by Ph.D.s who teach in the MBA programs in some of the finest schools in the country. A team of business editors from *The New York Times*— Mike Levitas, Tom Redburn, Brent Bowers, and James Schembari—provided their own expertise to edit a reference series that is beyond compare.

The New York Times Pocket MBA Series offers quick-reference key points learned in top MBA programs. The 25-key structure of each volume presents an unparalleled synopsis of crucial principles of specific areas of business expertise. The unique approach to this series packages academic books for consumers in an easy-to-use trade format that is ideal for the individual businessperson as well as an excellent training reference manual. Be sure to get all 12 titles in the series to complete your own MBA education.

Joseph Mills
Senior Managing Editor
Lebhar-Friedman Books

The New York Times Pocket MBA
Series includes these 12 volumes:

Analyzing Financial Statements

Business Planning

Business Financing

Growing & Managing a Business

Organizing a Company

Forecasting Budgets

Tracking & Controlling Costs

Sales & Marketing

Managing Investment

Going Global

Leadership & Vision

The Board of Directors

25 KEYS TO UNDERSTANDING THE NUMBERS

CONTENTS

KEY 1

Accounting is not a four-letter word

A ccounting is not a four-letter word. But to listen to many people faced with trying to understand what's presented in corporate annual reports, you might think so.

It doesn't have to be that way. Accounting is simply a system for recording and measuring the results of economic activity. It has proved durable because it is useful. Don't be intimidated just because you have not yet learned all the secrets. Managers, investors, and other stakeholders employ financial statements—the product of applying the rules of accounting—to monitor company performance, estimate returns on investment, establish business valuations, and decide whether to extend credit.

Those who run businesses must plan in advance using budgets. They set product prices, and decide whether to buy a part from a supplier or make it internally. All these activities, and many more, depend on interpreting accounting numbers.

Indeed, business is built on a foundation of numbers. The blueprint for understanding how a company is constructed—what has happened to it, when it happened and whether it can happen again—lies in the financial statements.

In this volume, I assume only that you are basically familiar with the workings of a business. The manual will be most useful for someone who has not been initiated into the mysteries of accounting, or for those who learned the rites long enough ago that memory has faded. After reading this book, you will grasp accounting terms and concepts that were previously obscure. You can then decipher the financial statements that once seemed to be written in hieroglyphics.

Throughout the keys, I refer to actual firms' financial reports, and provide World Wide Web addresses (URLs) for finding this information online. I recommend that you make frequent reference to these sites, as they will illuminate points in the text and deepen your understanding. You will appreciate what the income statement, balance sheet, footnotes, and other disclosures reveal by practicing speaking their language.

At the waning of the twentieth century, there is doubt in some circles that the numbers in financial statements have much meaningful relation to stock prices. Other experts wonder, in an era when Internet companies like Amazon.com are worth billions on paper despite not having earned a dime, if earnings are still useful for valuation. What we can say with certainty is the practice of accounting, and the use of financial information, have the strong imprimatur of time. The customs of accounting date back to before the Roman era. I predict they will be with us at least as long again.

KEY 2

Financial statements rely on fact, not possibility

A ccounting follows rules. It is important to understand who writes the rules and what they imply.

The Securities and Exchange Commission (SEC), in conjunction with the Financial Accounting Standards Board (FASB), sets accounting policy in the United States. It is known as GAAP, which stands for Generally Accepted Accounting Principles. The SEC requires that companies offering shares to the public make financial information available, which they do by publishing financial statements. Financial statements describe the firm's financial position, and the results of its operating, investing, and financing activities.

GAAP uses historical cost and accrual accounting to measure economic activity. Historical cost accounting registers events based on the economic value observed when a transaction is completed. A transaction is an exchange that transfers

Money isn't everything, but lack of your money isn't anything.

Franklin P. Adams, The Algonquin Wits

value between unrelated parties. (Within a company, a transaction records transfers of value between parts of the firm.) These values are carried forward in a firm's financial statements, unchanged unless a future transaction affects the item. Thus, even if subsequent events increase the market price of an item in inventory, its book value is not adjusted to reflect market conditions.

For example, assume the Old Times Corporation purchased in 1986 the land under a new building it was constructing. The site was in a then-remote business park, and the firm paid $390,000 for 1.2 acres. It also paid $280,000 for an adjoining three-quarter acre parcel for possible future expansion. By 1998, the park was bustling, no longer remote, and there were few remaining building sites. A property similar to the three-quarter acre lot recently had sold for $1,500,000.

Clearly, the vacant parcel represents an asset the company controls with a market value of about $1.5 million. Its value as reflected on the company's books, however, will still be $280,000—the original purchase price. This is a consequence of the GAAP requirement to use historical cost.

Until there is a completed transaction involving the parcel, the firm's books will not reflect any appreciation in value. A transaction is regarded as complete when title passes, and something of value is exchanged. Thus, historical cost is useful in maintaining objectivity. Why? As the saying goes, many's the slip 'twixt the cup and lip. GAAP wants to see a signed contract on the table before a transaction is recognized. Financial statements record events that actually take place, not those that might or could occur.

Does this imply that financial statements are flawed because they do not reflect current market values? Not at all. Old Times' managers and stockholders are obviously not prepared to sell the property for $280,000 just because that amount is reflected on the financial statements. Instead, knowledgeable users understand that financial statements use an historical cost basis. If current values are needed, call in appraisers!

GAAP also requires the use of accrual accounting for corporate financial statements. Accrual accounting affects financial statements when transactions are complete, but cash collection is not required.

To see this, suppose that in November 1999, Devon Bancshares offered to buy Old Times' vacant parcel for $1,650,000. After negotiations, Devon made a down payment of $250,000 on December 12, and gave Old Times a note secured by the property for $1,400,000. Devon, a company with an excellent credit history, will pay the balance over eight years, at 8 percent, beginning in January 2000. How should Old Times record the event?

Title has passed, and value has been exchanged. Thus, the transaction will be recognized in 1999. Although Old Times collected only $250,000 cash, the $1.4 million note receivable represents cash it is quite likely to receive over the next eight years. The accrual method reflects the parcel sale for $1.65 million on the 1999 income statement. Concurrently, the $280,000 cost of the lot will be matched against the $1.65 million revenue to show a gain of $1.37 million on the sale.

To summarize, because the sale was consummated in 1999, the financial statements reflect the $1.37 million gain in 1999. Value recognition is based upon the accrual rules for recognition, not when cash is collected.

Finally, we should note that GAAP is conservative. If the market price of an acquired item increases, historical cost accounting does not adjust the book value to reflect market conditions. The converse, however, is not true. If the market price of an acquired item declines notably, the book value should be reduced.

A write down reflects the conservatism in GAAP—its tendency to avoid overstating value. While GAAP generally ignores appreciation of value until there is a completed transaction, a measurable decline is recognized in the period it occurs. Under GAAP, overstating the realizable value of assets is perceived as a greater evil than injecting an element of the hypothetical into financial statements.

KEY 3

What's hanging in the balance sheet?

The balance sheet reports a firm's financial position at a given moment. It portrays the basic accounting equation:

Assets = Liabilities + Owners' equity

To understand the equation, we need to define its terms. Assets (A) represent valuable rights and properties a firm controls. Examples of assets include cash, accounts receivable, inventory, property and equipment, and patents.

Liabilities (L) are the firm's future obligations to sacrifice value, and arise from past transactions the firm entered into with suppliers, creditors, and employees. Accounts payable, wages and taxes payable, long-term debt, leases, and pensions are all liabilities.

Owners' equity (OE) depicts stockholders' residual interest; that is, what is left after liabilities are subtracted from assets (A − L). OE accounts include common stock, preferred stock, retained earnings, and treasury stock.

The balance sheet thus presents a picture of what the firm controls, and what claims exist against the firm's assets. Each balance sheet category is measured according to GAAP, as of the financial statement date. By convention, assets are shown either on the left side or upper part of the page; liabilities and owners' equity are presented on the right side, or lower part of the page.

The balance sheet is classified according to liquidity. How close is a particular item to generating cash, in the case of assets? When will cash or value be sacrificed, we ask for liabilities? Assets are classified as current if the receipt of cash is expected within the next year. Liabilities are current if the obligation to pay cash or sacrifice value falls within a year.

Assets that provide the firm its productive capacity, enabling it to produce goods or to deliver services, are classified as long-term assets; they will not be turned into cash in the near future. Long-term liabilities are claims a company will not have to meet during the current year.

For example, inventory is a current asset. Presumably, inventory will be sold in short order. Either cash is collected, or, if a customer receives credit, an account receivable is created. Typically, an account receivable is collected within a month or two—at which point, the firm realizes cash.

Similarly, accounts payable is a current liability. Accounts payable is created when a firm deals with suppliers who extend credit. Because the obligation to repay is due within a month or so, accounts payable is a current liability.

We've discussed the basic accounting equation, and how assets, liabilities, and owners' equity are defined. To understand what it reports, let's examine 3M's balance sheet from its annual report (www.3M.com) for December 31, 1998. In Key 2, I explained that GAAP mostly measures economic activity by historical cost. This is a fair approximation, but it oversimplifies how financial statements are actually prepared. We shall see there are several valuation approaches that guide balance sheet reporting.

The first thing to observe is that the balance sheet is indeed in balance. The total of the assets (left side) and liabilities and owners' equity (right side) is $14.153 billion. Since A = L + OE, we're clear to proceed and discuss selected accounts. A user should reflect on the various account balances only after reading the pertinent footnotes (more about that in Key 10).

Among 3M's Current Assets are cash, accounts receivable, and inventories. None of these items is reported at exactly its historical cost amount. 3M held $211 million in cash and cash equivalents. If the cash were only U.S. dollars, the amount would reflect balances based on historical values. 3M, however, runs foreign operations. Its footnotes tell us that foreign currencies are translated at year-end exchange rates. Thus, the cash account comingles historical cost with current market-value accounting.

Net Accounts Receivable total $2.666 billion. The term "net" indicates the dollar amount of gross accounts receivable was reduced to an estimate of the cash that will be collected. 3M actually had $2.751 billion of receivables; $2.666 billion represents the net value expected after subtracting $85 million of doubtful accounts.

Minnesota Mining and Manufacturing Co.
Balance Sheet at December 31, 1998 (dollars in millions)

Assets

Current Assets

Cash & marketable securities	$211
Other securities	237
Accounts receivable — net	2,666
Inventories	2,219
Other current assets	985
Total Current Assets	**$6,318**
Investments	623
Property, plant & equipment — net	5,566
Other Assets	1,646
Total	**$14,153**

Liabilities & Stockholders' Equity

Current Liabilities

Accounts payable	$868
Accrued payroll	487
Income taxes payable	261
Short-term debt	1,492
Other current liabilities	1,278
Total Current Liabilities	**$4,386**
Other liabilities	2,217
Long-term debt	1,614
Stockholders' equity — net	5,936
Total	**$14,153**

3M disclosed $2.219 billion of inventories. These are reported at cost or market, whichever is lower. The value displayed is based on historical cost, but has been reduced somewhat because obsolescence and spoilage are expected to diminish its value.

Thus we see that historical cost is sometimes modified. Estimates adjust values to avoid overstating the amount of cash that will be realized. And there are other examples of deviation from historical cost.

3M reported $860 million of current and non-current Securities and Investments ($237 plus $623) for 1998 in its footnotes. Management disclosed that $164 million of the investments are to be held until they mature. According to GAAP, such holdings are shown at historical cost, adjusted for any premium or discount to face value paid when the security was acquired. Another $696 million of investments is available for sales, but these receive different treatment. Since they might be sold, they are reported at market value. Any gains and losses beyond historical cost affect the company owners' equity accounts. Thus, Management's intention for investments affects the values reported.

The company is showing over $5.5 billion of net Property, Plant, and Equipment (PPE). This represents the long-term assets that provide productive capacity. The net aspect has to do with the subtraction of accumulated depreciation from PPE. Key 17 goes into detail about depreciation expense. In essence, depreciation is a method for spreading the cost of owning PPE over the useful lives of the components. It is not an adjustment intended to reflect PPE at market value! As such, the net PPE account reflects a mixture of historical cost and accounting estimations.

Moving to the right side of the balance sheet, we can say that the Current Liabilities are reflected at historical cost. Further, because the current liabilities will be settled in the near future, the amounts also approximate market value. Long-term Debt and Other Liabilities are a different story. The

1998 footnotes show hundreds of millions of dollars of Euronotes, Eurobonds, and other debt that matures over the next ten years. Since the coupon rates on the notes are fixed, the market values of these debts vary as worldwide-borrowing conditions change. The debt is carried on the balance sheet at amounts that may not reflect current value.

Similarly, Stockholders' Equity is reported at its book value, which is not necessarily the same as the market value for control of the firm (as reflected in the stock market). Market values represent economic expectations; book values reflect the aggregation of the GAAP requirements and historical cost orientation we have been discussing. Key 9 will describe more about stockholders' equity.

To summarize, the balance sheet, following the rules laid out under GAAP, portrays what the firm owns, and the claims on assets from creditors and owners. In later keys, you will learn how GAAP overlooks certain economic aspects. Balance sheet values are not necessarily market values.

KEY 4

Take steps to understand the income statement

The income statement reports the results of a firm's operations for a period of time (in contrast to the balance sheet, which portrays financial position at a specific point in time). The balance sheet reports levels of assets, liabilities, and stockholders' equity. The income statement reports changes in levels (or flows).

The flows reported in the income statement are expressed in terms of revenues and expenses. According to Statement of Financial Accounting Concepts No. 6 (1985), revenues are:

> "inflows of assets . . . from delivering or producing goods, rendering services, or other activities that are the company's ongoing major or central operations."

What does that mean? If a company engages in operating activity that leads to an increase in its assets, it recognizes it as revenue. But an inflow of assets alone is not sufficient. It is the type of activity that is critical.

For example, imagine that Zeta Company, a telecommunications consulting firm, receives a $45,000 credit to its checking account when it opens a line of credit at Alpha Bank. Clearly, assets flowed into the firm, but this flow is not revenue. The transaction reflects asset inflows associated with an increase in a liability. Zeta now owes the bank $45,000. To recognize revenue, Zeta must undertake consulting activity.

Expenses are similarly defined. Expenses are outflows of assets (or increases in liabilities) associated with the production of goods, or rendering of services. The next key discusses matching, a central GAAP concept in properly determining expenses.

Revenue is recognized when two conditions are met. First, the process of delivering or producing goods, or providing service, is substantially complete. Second, cash collection is reasonably certain. That occurs when a firm receives cash, or when it receives a claim (e.g., note receivable) that ultimately can be realized as cash.

Income statements also present information on two critical, additional items: gains and losses. While revenues and expenses are associated with operations, gains and losses arise from non-operational or incidental activity. To be sure, gains and losses affect owners' equity as much as revenues and expenses. But they reflect events like exchanges of capital assets (selling equipment for a price greater than its book value or losses on closing a plant). Non-operating events also including the effects of holding assets and liabilities while their market values change (writing down obsolete inventory, for example). Last, non-operating items include the impact of events beyond the firm's control (such as fire or flood damage, or awards in lawsuits).

About two-thirds of public firms present their income statements in what is called the multi-step format. To examine this, let's look at a summary of Sears' (sears.com) 1995 income statement (numbers are in millions, except for earnings per share data). Sears ends its reporting year on the last Saturday in December, which was December 30 in 1995.

Sears Income Statement for the Year Ending December 30, 1995	
Revenue	$34,835
Cost of goods sold	$23,160
Gross profit	$11,675
Operating expenses:	
Selling & administrative expenses	8,008
Interest & uncollectible accounts	1,962
Operating income:	$1,705
Other income	23
Income before taxes	1,728
Income taxes	703
Income from continuing operations	$1,025
Discontinued operations (net of taxes)	776
Net income	$1,801
Earnings per share-basic	$4.55
Earnings per share-diluted	$4.50

You can see that the income statement reported Sears' 1995 results in steps. The approach first presented Revenue, Cost of Goods Sold and Gross Profit. Its Gross Profit (i.e., Revenue minus Cost of Goods Sold) of $11.7 billion was available to cover operating costs. Sears then deducted other operating expenses, reported other income items, and arrived at Income from Continuing Operations of $1.7 billion. After paying taxes of $700 million, it earned $1 billion from its ongoing activity. Last, there was a positive effect from the operations of Allstate—which footnote 2 of Sears'

1995 annual report tells us was in the process of being divested, shown in Discontinued Operations. Allstate's contribution was $776 million after taxes, and Sears' net income was $1.8 billion. The income statement gets to net earnings in steps, reporting the revenue and expense associated with each stage.

Two other important items appear on the statement, as Sears reported its earnings per share (EPS). Basic EPS represents net income divided by the average number of shares of common stock. Diluted EPS considers the hypothetical effect of converting all securities and instruments with equity claims (e.g., stock options) into common stock. Generally, Diluted EPS will be less than Basic EPS.

KEY 5

Matching and adjusting— the crux of accrual accounting

The accrual method specifies that expenses— the value sacrificed in acquiring assets for resale, in producing goods, or providing services—should be matched against revenue during the period in which revenue is recognized. Matching is an essential feature of accrual accounting, and is a major difference between cash basis and accrual approaches. One of the principal ways accountants implement matching is through adjusting journal entries. Adjusting entries affect the financial statement accounts before they are closed for the reporting period.

Consider this example. Every three months, Shirley Pall, the accountant for Brasserie Katz, prepares financial statements for the restaurant. At the end of the period, Ms. Pall balances the books and prepares adjustments. We can learn about matching by considering some common situations that require adjusting.

The Brasserie has a calendar-based fiscal year

(January 1–December 31). Felix Katz pays his staff each Friday for work through Thursday. In 1999, the last day of the first quarter of the fiscal year (March 31) fell on Wednesday. The restaurant owed six days wages to employees (March 26 through March 31); the next payday was April 2.

To match the six days of wages against the revenues from the quarter, Ms. Pall made an adjusting entry. She charged Wage Expense, and set up Wages Payable, a liability for the unpaid wages. This adjustment registers unrecorded expenses.

The Brasserie renewed its liability insurance in February, when Mr. Katz wrote a check for the premium for six months (February 1 through July 31). At the end of March, four months of coverage remained. When the accountant was closing the books, she made an entry to adjust for the prepaid expenses. She charged Insurance Expense for the two months of insurance that was used up, and reduced an asset account Prepaid Insurance, to balance the entry.

On March 30, Sherry Brush, a well-to-do exporter, reserved the Brasserie by giving Mr. Katz a $1,500 deposit for a banquet she's planning to hold in May. The accountant treated the transaction as unearned revenue. The $1,500 is an advance against future sales. As such, the Brasserie has a liability to deliver food service and hospitality in May. Ms. Pall made a bookkeeping entry that picked up the increase in cash, and recognized the future obligation.

There is one last adjustment she made for unrecorded revenue. Three years ago, Mr. Katz sold some surplus kitchen equipment to Brentwood Partners. Brentwood paid $36,000 cash, and signed a five-year, $200,000 note that requires semi-annual interest and principal payments to Brasserie Katz. The next payment is due April 1. Although the Brasserie received no payment during the current three-month period (the last payment was made in October), three additional months of interest accumulated. While no cash changed hands, Brentwood's interest obligation increased $9,000. To reflect this, Ms. Pall increases the Interest Receivable account, and also increases Interest Revenue. Interest revenue ceases to be unrecorded after this adjustment.

If you can count your money, you don't have a billion dollars.

J. Paul Getty, International Herald Tribune

KEY 6

Who decides what financial statements contain?

Financial statements are prepared according to Generally Accepted Accounting Principles. GAAP is the body of authoritative pronouncements, rules, and conventions that shape the practice of accounting. The purpose of GAAP is to ensure that a firm's financial statements faithfully represent its operating results and economic circumstances.

Remember that GAAP is transaction oriented. Financial statements record events when an exchange occurs, but other things that affect the value of a firm happen without exchanges. For example, an increase in the know-how of employees adds to value; so does creation or improvement in the good will of customers toward the firm. Yet neither phenomenon is an event that GAAP records. GAAP in general does not attempt to value these intangible assets. I discuss the implication of these issues in Key 13.

In 1934, Congress granted the Securities and

Exchange Commission authority to determine accounting practice in the United States. The SEC requires every publicly-held company to file a Form 10-K—an annual report that contains audited financial statements, plus Management's Discussion and Analysis of results and significant developments—within 90 days of the end of the fiscal year. (A fiscal year is a firm's 12-month reporting year, and thus need not begin in January.) Form 10-Q, an unaudited set of financial statements which also includes a management discussion of results, is due 45 days after each quarter. The SEC also mandates that firms file a Form 8-K if significant events occur, such as an acquisition or divestiture, a bankruptcy filing, a change in auditors, or a resignation of any directors.

Besides prescribing the frequency and form of financial reporting, the SEC also has set a number of accounting policies. The SEC, for example, initiated the disclosure of more detailed data on business segments, reporting of oil and gas reserves, and the effects of inflation. Still, the SEC has generally allowed the private sector to determine GAAP.

The Financial Accounting Standards Board (FASB) is the independent, seven-member group that has set accounting standards since 1973. The FASB disseminates information about emerging issues, receives reports from its watchdog committees and comments from the public, and debates and deliberates extensively before enacting new requirements. To protect their independence, FASB members, who serve five-year terms, sever all ties to their former CPA firms, corporations, governments, and universities.

Only the FASB and SEC can create GAAP. The SEC

and the American Institute of Certified Public Accountants (AICPA) regard FASB pronouncements as authoritative. Both the FASB and SEC monitor the business environment for reporting problems and changes in industry and technology that require new accounting treatments.

For example, corporations' use of complex financial instruments (swaps, futures, and options) exploded in the 1990s. Statement of Financial Accounting Standards No. 105 (1990) deals with disclosing off-balance sheet risk; SFAS No. 107 (1991) discusses fair value disclosures for financial instruments; and SFAS No. 133 (1998) considers how to account for derivatives and hedging. Given the objective that financial statements be fair representations of financial position, GAAP evolves as business conditions change.

While specific FASB pronouncements are detailed and technical, the FASB objectives for financial statements are clear. They are stated in Statement of Financial Accounting Concepts No. 2. The objectives include relevance, timeliness, representational faithfulness, reliability, verifiability, and comparability.

Relevance and timeliness are crucial for investor decision making. Representational faithfulness implies that financial statements characterize a firm's performance and financial position fairly and accurately. Reliability and verifiability lend credibility to financial statements. Comparability permits users to assess financial statements from different companies, or to evaluate one firm's statements over time

KEY 7

Where cash came from and where it went

The Statement of Cash Flows (SOCF) reports which activities generated cash and how it was used.

Managers make operating, investing, and financing decisions that affect cash flow. Operating decisions concern what the firm makes, how it makes it, and how it sells it. Organizing production or services, marketing, and administration are the provinces of operations.

Investing decisions concern how a firm uses its capital. What assets provide the firm's productive capacity? Will the factory use robots? Does the shop floor have separate stations for drill presses and lathes? Will short-term cash be held in checking or money-market accounts? These are investing decisions.

How does a company obtain capital? Does it factor receivables, offer medium-term notes, or sell equity? Does it pay owners dividends, or retain cash for reinvestment in the business? Does the firm buy long-term assets, or lease them? These are financing issues.

Clearly, the decisions managers make are interrelated. If Green Industries decides to make running shoes in a Bangladesh factory, it can forego installing robots in its New Hampshire plant. The

Finance is the art of passing currency from hand to hand until it finally disappears.

Robert W. Sarnoff

decision on how to operate affects how to invest. Despite such complications, SFAS No. 95 (1987) requires a firm to report the cash effects in each of the three domains of management activity.

SFAS No. 95 requires the SOCF (along with the balance sheet, income statement, and statement of stockholders' equity) as part of the minimum package of financial disclosures. Firms must choose to present the SOCF using either the direct or indirect approach.

Under the direct approach, firms report specific cash receipts and disbursements within the category of Cash Provided by Operations. SFAS No. 95 suggests companies disclose cash collections from customers, interest and dividends received from other companies, payments to employees and suppliers, taxes and interest paid, and other operating payments.

Under the indirect approach, firms adjust net income to derive Cash Provided by Operations. GAAP requires accrual accounting for corporations' financial reporting. As discussed in Keys 1 and 5, the accrual process does not require that cash be received or sacrificed before revenues and expenses can be recorded. Thus, under the indirect approach, all items that did not generate cash are subtracted from revenues. Any expense items that did not require expenditure of cash are added back.

That's the theory. In the next key, we'll examine Merck's 1998 SOCF and discuss how to interpret it.

KEY 8

Monetary matters need not be murky. Follow the cash

Although SFAS No. 95 recommends that companies use the direct approach in preparing the Statement of Cash Flows (SOCF), over 90 percent of public firms use the indirect approach. One reason is that the direct approach requires firms to produce additional data. The 1998 annual report of Merck and Co., a large pharmaceutical company, offers a good opportunity to study a SOCF prepared using the indirect method. We will see it provides a wealth of information that is not reported elsewhere.

Merck & Co., Inc. and Subsidiaries Year Ended December 31, 1998 ($ in millions)	
Cash Flow from Operating Activities	
Income before taxes	$8,133.1
Adjustments to reconcile Income before taxes to cash provided by operations	
Acquired research	1,039.5
Gains on sales of businesses	(2,147.7)
Depreciation and amortization	1,015.1

Other	156.6
Net changes in assets and liabilities	(741.7)
Cash provided by operations before taxes	**7,454.9**
Income taxes paid	(2,126.6)
Net cash provided by operating activities	**$5,328.3**
Cash Flow from Investing Activities	
Capital expenditures	(1,973.4)
Purchase of securities, subsidiaries and other investments	(29,675.4)
Proceeds from sale of securities, subsidiaries and other investments	28,618.9
Proceeds from sales of businesses	2,586.2
Other	432.3
Net cash flow from investing activities	**(11.4)**
Cash Flow from Financing Activities	
Net change in short-term borrowings	(457.2)
Proceeds from issuance of debt	2,379.5
Payments on debt	(340.6)
Purchase of treasury stock	(3,625.5)
Dividends paid to stockholders	(2,253.1)
Proceeds from exercise of stock options	490.1
Other	(114.1)
Net cash flow from financing activities	**(3,920.9)**
Effect of exchange rate changes on cash	
and cash equivalents	85.1
Net increase in cash and cash equivalents	1,481.1
Cash and cash equivalents at beginning of year	1,125.1
Cash and cash equivalents at end of year	$2,606.2

Merck's SOCF tells us why and how cash changed in 1998. The statement begins with income before taxes of $8.133 billion. Depreciation expense reduced income, but didn't cost Merck any cash. (The cash was expended when capital investments were made.) Thus $1.015 billion of depreciation is added back.

Gains on businesses that were sold are $2.148 (let's state amounts in billions), but these are bookkeeping entries that, like depreciation, do not generate cash. They are thus subtracted; the proceeds from the sales of business show up in the Investing section. Acquired research is an item charged to expense when Merck acquired R&D firms. The associated cash shows up in the Investing section; in Operations, we must add back the charge. After paying out $2.127 for income taxes, Merck's operating activity contributed $5.328 billion for 1998.

The investing section shows us where capital was used. Merck spent $1.973 on new equipment and facilities. The major investing activities were the transactions described as Purchase or sale of securities, subsidiaries, and other investments. Footnotes 3, 4, 5, and 10 in its financial statements discuss Merck's divestitures, joint ventures, and affiliates. The net effect of its extensive activities is a cash outflow of $1.056 billion ($28.619 inflow from sales less $29.675 outflow from purchases). Merck also realized $2.586 from outright sales of business lines. The net effect of all investing transactions was an outflow of cash of $11.4 million.

The financing activity section reports how Merck raised capital. Note that both inflows of capital ($2.379 from issuing debt) and outflows ($.341 to redeem maturing debt) are presented. GAAP requires that both inflow and outflow effects of transactions be reported in the investing and financing sections, rather than the net effect of the transaction.

The bulk of cash outflows for financing was from purchase of stock on the open market (treasury stock for $3.625) and payment of cash dividends ($2.253). The company realized $490 million from employees who exercised their incentive stock options. Because Merck repurchased so much stock, the net impact of financing activities is an outflow of $3.921 billion in cash.

Overall favorable exchange rate changes added $85 million to Merck's cash. At the end of 1997, Merck had $1.125 billion. For 1998, the effects of operating, investing, and financing activities increased cash by $1.481 billion, so that $2.606 billion is the amount of Cash and Cash Equivalents as of December 31, 1998. The cash reported on Merck's balance sheet confirms this.

Money is like muck, not

good except it be spread.

Francis Bacon, **Of Seditions and Troubles**

KEY 9

Keeping owners' claims straight

The Statement of Changes in Stockholders' Equity lists the accounts included in owners' equity on the balance sheet. These accounts represent shareowners' interests in the business, measured using book value. To understand what it tells us, we'll turn again to 3M's 1998 annual report. From the balance sheet in Key 3, we see Stockholders' Net Equity as of the end of 1998 is $5.936 billion. Let's examine what caused the components of stockholders' equity to increase $10 million since the end of 1997.

The column, Common Stock and Capital in Excess of Par, represents contributed capital. This is the value of cash or other assets the company has received in exchange for shares of ownership (stock). Companies often issue two types of stock: Preferred and common. Preferred stockholders are paid their dividends before common stockholders. Upon liquidation of the corporation, common stockholders receive whatever is left after debt owners and preferred stockholders have been paid. 3M's footnote (page 36) tells us the firm has never issued preferred stock. In many states, securities laws require corporations to establish a minimum value per share of stock. This is known as the stock's par value. A corporation records the par value of stock issued in one account, and any amounts received above that in a separate account, Capital in Excess of Par (also called additional paid-in capital). For 3M, we can calculate from page 36 of its annual report that there are 472 million shares with a par value of $236 million ($.50 per share), and that Capital in Excess of Par is $60 million. This gives us $296 million, the total of column two.

Retained Earnings represents the aggregate total of Net Income for the years the company has been in existence, less all dividends paid. You can trace 3M's 1998 net income from the Income Statement to the Retained Earnings column of the Statement of Changes in Stockholders' Equity. While net income increased retained earnings, cash dividends of $2.20 per share reduced 3M's retained earnings by $887 million.

In addition to cash dividends, firms issue stock dividends, in which each shareholder receives additional shares in proportion to his holdings. For example, if a 5 percent stock dividend is declared, a shareholder with 20 shares receives one additional share. Contributed capital will increase by the value of the stock issued, and retained earnings will decrease the same amount. Stock splits, though similar, receive a different accounting treatment. The par value of all shares is adjusted, but contributed capital and retained earnings remain the same. Thus, in a two-for-one split, par value is cut in half, and a shareholder with 20 shares receives 20 more.

Minnesota Mining and Manufacturing Co. 1998 Statement of Changes in Stockholders' Equity (dollars in millions)		
	Total	Common Stock and Capital in Excess of Par
Balance at December 31, 1997	$5,926	$296
Net income	1,175	
Cumulative translation - net	29	
Fair value adjustments	2	
Dividends paid ($2.20 per share)	(887)	
Amortization of unearned compensation	29	
Reacquired stock (7.4 million shares)	(618)	
Issuances pursuant to stock option		
and benefit plans (4.6 million shares)	280	
Balance at December 31, 1998	$5,936	$296

Companies sometimes use excess cash to repurchase stock in the open market. The repurchased stock is known as treasury stock, and is reported at cost as a subtraction from stockholders' equity. Treasury stock often is used to provide the shares for employees' stock options. In addition, since no dividends are paid on stock while it is in the treasury, repurchasing stock has the effect of increasing earnings per share. Upon reissue, an adjustment is made to capital in excess of par or retained earnings for the difference between the repurchase cost and the proceeds. In 1998, notice that 3M repurchased 7.4 million of its own shares for $618 million, and reissued 4.6 million shares that cost $436 million (sold to employees for incentive awards at a discount of $156 million). As a result, retained earnings was reduced $338 million.

The statement's fifth column adjusts owners' equity for accounting effects of 3M's Employee Stock Ownership Plan (ESOP), which provides

Retained Earnings	Treasury Stock	Unearned Compensation ESOP	Accumulated Other Comprehensive Income
$9,848	$(3,300)	$(379)	$(539)
1,175			
			29
			2
(887)			
		29	
	(618)		
(156)	436		
$9,980	$(3,482)	$(350)	$(508)

employees a tax-advantaged way to acquire shares of their own company, usually at a discount The final column balance concerns Comprehensive Income items. There is a foreign currency translation adjustment of ($518 million) and an unrealized gain on investments of $10 million (per page 36). 3M values its foreign currencies at year-end exchange rates. If the yen buys fewer dollars this year compared to last year, then 3M's Japan assets (translated from yen to dollars) will decrease. Over its history, 3M has had a loss of $518 million from exchange rate fluctuations, although in 1998 it had a gain of $29 million.

In Key 3, you learned that 3M owns $696 million of securities and investments, reported at market value because they are available for sale. The excess of the market value over cost, known as the unrealized gain, is included in stockholders' equity. On December 31, 1998 the market value of 3M's investment was $10 million higher than its cost.

The last row of the statement depicts the net effects. Summing the columns, you can see that Stockholders Contributed Capital and Retained Earnings are more than $10 billion. This interest is reduced by Treasury Stock, ESOP claims, and Comprehensive Income adjustments. At the end of 1998, the net book value of Stockholder claims on 3M assets is nearly $6 billion.

KEY 10

Don't ignore the fine print! Read the footnotes

Footnotes explain and elaborate the summarized information presented in the financial statements. They are an integral part of the presentation of results. Auditors are required to evaluate the disclosures in footnotes for accuracy and conformity to GAAP as part of the audit process. A firm's financial position cannot be properly understood without reading the footnotes. Why is this so?

At any company, management adopts a strategy for financial reporting, either intentionally or by default (see Key 11). Accounting choices and estimates have varying effects on financial statements. Some tend to increase income (aggressive reporting), others decrease income (conservative reporting), and yet other choices are considered neutral.

To understand a given firm's strategy, you must study the accounting policies disclosed in the footnotes, see how they affect the balance sheet and income statement, and compare them with the approach followed by its competitors.

We can appreciate the importance of footnotes by observing the relative space they occupy in the annual report. For example, AT&T's 1995 report (www.att.com) contains four pages of financial statements and 13 pages of footnotes, while Wal-Mart's 1996 report (www.wal-mart.com) presents four pages of statements and six pages of footnotes.

Footnotes illuminate the facts and circumstances underlying the balance sheet, income statement, cash flow statement, and owners' equity statement. For example, why did AT&T pay tax at an effective rate of 85 percent—far higher than the U.S. corporate rate of 35 percent? Footnote 9 from 1995 explains the rate arose from heavy foreign taxation associated with operational restructuring.

Footnotes address four general areas. First, they disclose a firm's accounting policies. This provides insight into the assumptions, estimates, and judgments that management makes. Say you want to understand how Wal-Mart's results compare with other retailers, like J.C. Penney or Sears. In retailing, inventory is a large component of total cost. The cost method chosen for inventory can affect the amount of cost reported. Footnote 1 in Wal-Mart's 1996 annual report discloses the firm used the last-in, first-out (LIFO) method (see Key 18). After collecting this information for the competitors, you can assess whether the financial statements are comparable, or require adjustment to a common basis.

Second, the footnotes augment the summary numbers found in the statements. The 1997 AT&T

balance sheet reports $6.8 billion of long-term debt. An investor or analyst needs to know when the obligations mature, because when debt comes due it places demands on cash flows. Footnote 11 in 1997 presents a schedule that provides data to estimate future scheduled cash payments for debt service.

What we now call "finance" is, I hold, an intellectual perversion of what began as warm human love.

Robert Graves, **Mammon**

Third, footnotes reveal important information that does not appear in the financial statements. Events that may occur, but as yet have not—called contingencies—are material facts that can affect investor decision-making. Since GAAP reporting is based on completed transactions, recognizing such contingencies on the balance sheet or income statement is unwarranted. The footnotes serve for disclosing such facts.

Finally, footnotes provide supplementary information required by the SEC and FASB. Such data assist a user in understanding the environment the firm operates in. Supplemental disclosures include segmenting a firm's revenue, operating income, and assets by industry classification.

General Electric (www.ge.com)—with total revenues of $91 billion—reported its business segments in 1997 in footnote 28. They include aircraft engines, appliances, broadcasting, industrial products, materials, power generation, technical products, financing, and specialty insurance. GE is hardly only a light bulb and refrigerator company; its largest segment is financial services! Footnote 29 reports operations by worldwide geographic divisions—United States, Europe, Pacific Basin, and other areas.

Footnotes also discuss the complex financial instruments held by a firm, and include a discussion of the risks the firm is exposed to from changes in interest rates and movements in foreign exchange markets. If you want a deeper understanding of what's going on, you must read the footnotes.

KEY 11

What shapes a firm's financial reporting strategy?

Firms compete in various markets for capital, customers, and employees. Financial statements provide information about a firm's financial position and operating results. Stakeholders—investors, lenders, employees, managers, suppliers, customers, and regulators—have an interest in the firm's financial status, and thus create a demand for information.

They use information to decide, for example, whether to buy the firm's shares, lend it capital, continue as employees, or increase the tax rate. From its own perspective, a firm has incentives to supply information, for reasons such as minimizing its cost of capital, securing the best terms from suppliers and lenders, or assuring customers it will be around to honor a guarantee.

Information is useful to stakeholders for projecting what the future holds for a particular company. But the level of knowledge and appreciation of the facts of a firm's situation differ between its

Business? It's quite simple:

it's other people's money

Alexandre Dumas

own managers and external parties. Consequently, the price of a company's stock might not fully reflect its potential value. This is a problem, called information asymmetry, which can be reduced by disclosure of financial information. Disclosure thus can affect firm value. Investors and other stakeholders may impose a discount in the presence of uncertainty, or offer a premium for a company known to have superior opportunities.

Disclosure also can impose costs on a firm. Certainly, a firm bears costs of collecting data, preparing, and disseminating financial reports, but these costs tend to be relatively small for firms of any significant size. More important is the potential to reveal proprietary information to competitors—gratuitously! There is also the possibility of litigation by disgruntled investors, who can assert damages from relying on misleading, or overly optimistic information. This is especially the case when firms make voluntary projections about the outcomes of future events.

In the United States, publicly-held firms are required to provide a minimum level of financial information by the Securities and Exchange Commission. Forms 10-K, 10-Q, and 8-K, as well as Proxy Statements and security registration statements give investors a look into a firm's internal workings. Before 1935, when the SEC began operating, the variation across firms' financial reports was much greater than it is today. Still, even apart from legal requirements, there are plenty of reasons why firms want to get information out to the public.

Imagine a world where disclosures are voluntary. Firms with lesser or even dismal prospects will tend to withhold some facts. Firms with better prospects will seek to distinguish themselves. If better firms are able to signal their superiority, they enjoy reduced capital costs, attract better employees, and sustain good relations with suppliers and customers. Greater disclosure and verifiable information can help separate a firm from the pack. Credibility is lent to a firm's financial disclosures by the auditor's examination and report, as well as by the criminal penalties imposed for fraudulent financial reporting.

Thus, a mixture of mandated requirements and disclosure incentives explain why firms in the United States provide financial statements. Firms must comply with the minimum reporting requirements, but have latitude to make additional disclosures. In turn, the possibility of litigation and a desire not to give away valuable proprietary information limit the level of voluntary disclosures. A good reporting strategy balances the benefits and costs of disclosure.

KEY 12

Financial reports are useful for both running and evaluating the company

B efore the results of a company's activities can be understood, they must be captured and measured. To answer the question, "How is the business doing?" we need tools to gauge performance. Managers, investors, and other stakeholders use financial reporting as one of the principal means for evaluation. Managers rely on financial reports to plan and monitor operations. An essential managerial exercise is comparing actual to budgeted results.

It is important for managers to understand and respond to deviations from expected performance. Both positive and negative variances (differences between actual results and the budget) should be examined. A rigorous budgeting and analysis process increases understanding of the business' dynamics. Better decision making flows from appropriate responses to significant variances.

Management's internal financial data are much

more detailed, and are generated more frequently than what is provided for external purposes. Sales, for example, can be put into categories by product, region, or customer. Accounting periods for managerial purposes are monthly, although some industries require weekly, daily or even hourly measurement. Thus, a resort might expect to be busier during critical vacation weeks, while a retailer wants to know if a daily or weekly sale is successful. At an even finer level, a commuter-train line or a telephone company can have intra-day concerns. For example, how does customer demand respond to time-of-day pricing schedules?

Internal financial reporting is shaped by the information requirements of managers. Managers decide to collect and analyze data when they believe the benefits of information exceed the costs.

In large firms, there are different needs at various levels of the company. The manager of a field office may be interested in billings per sales representative to see if sales quotas were met. Meanwhile, a senior executive in the same enterprise has a broader perspective. She may concern herself with Divisional Revenue classified by local currency to assess foreign exchange exposure, or consider how differences in strategies between divisions affect results.

Internal financial reports are also used in investing decisions. When evaluating the purchase of an expensive laborsaving machine versus a proposal to run a second shift, for instance, a plant manager should consider the expected impact on the company's financial results. Meanwhile, on a broader level, senior managers seek to expand the most profitable and fastest-growing parts of the company by directing more resources to the activity. Profitability measures such as return on investment or the rate of earnings growth are used to identify opportunities.

Stock options and bonus plans help align executives' incentives with corporate objectives. Executive-performance evaluations frequently use financial statement numbers. Return on investment, profit margin, and sales growth are common performance parameters. If a corporate goal is to increase profitability through cost reductions, then a manager should be rewarded for a reduction in division overhead. The reward could be a bonus based on the increase in profit margin.

Outside the firm, external stakeholders rely on the financial statements as their primary source of detailed financial information. Prudent investors examine the financial statements, in combination with other sources of information, to assess a company's prospects. If the financial statements reveal deterioration in performance or other troubling signs, a prospective stockholder may decide not to invest. Alternatively, positive information might encourage investors to put their money into the firm.

Banks and suppliers examine financial statements when deciding whether to extend credit. They are interested in a prospect's creditworthiness. Their concerns include net current assets, liquidity, and profitability—all essential to assure that debts are paid and suppliers receive timely payment. Asset-based creditors may use the balance sheet to consider the adequacy of their security interests in accounts receivable, inventory or, in the case of a mortgagor, a building.

There are still more users of financial statements.

Equity analysts on Wall Street closely monitor public companies on behalf of their clients. Their earnings forecasts are closely followed, and often are reported in the business press. Customers may be interested in their suppliers' financial stability. After all, they will be depending on an assured source of supply and want to know that it will be available in the future. Government authorities and regulators review financial statements when auditing a tax return or considering elements of public policy. Labor unions often prepare for contract negotiations by assessing employer profitability and liquidity.

You may fall into any of these categories.

When it comes to finances, remember that there are no withholding taxes on the wages of sin.

Mae West, **Last Word**

KEY 13

Financial statements have trouble measuring future opportunities properly

---

Because GAAP is focused on what has already occurred, financial statements might not measure future opportunities properly. What about transactions that have implications for future changes in value that are presently unclear? How do financial statements represent them?

To answer these questions, we need to learn about intangible assets. Intangibles are non-physical assets having unknown useful lives. Companies can create or acquire intangible assets that GAAP does not recognize. A good example is the treatment of Research and Development costs. R&D are aimed at discovering and implementing knowledge to be used for selling new products or achieving cost savings in the future. Under SFAS No. 2, R&D are expensed as incurred. Let's consider the implications of this policy as it affects Lucent Technologies.

Lucent (lucent.com), a spin-off from AT&T, is a

company involved in managing data, optical networking, and wireless systems. The company's future is based upon its ability to discover new technologies, and to innovate in employing technology, which it undertakes through its Bell Laboratories division. The name Lucent gave to its 1998 annual report, "At the Center of the Communications Revolution," tells you how the company sees itself.

In 1998, Lucent had revenues of $30.1 billion and net income of $970 million. Its Cash Flow from Operations was $1.4 billion, and it spent $3.7 billion on R&D costs. Clearly, R&D play a crucial part in what Lucent does. For every $8 of revenue it received in 1998, the firm invested $1 on research and development.

Remember, as Key 4 explained, that expenses are outflows of assets. In other words, expenses are recorded when assets are used up. Treating all $3.7 billion Lucent spent on R&D as an expense implies that the benefits of 1998's R&D effort occur only in 1998. Clearly that is not the case. The benefits extend to future periods, although which periods benefit and to what extent is uncertain.

Because of the difficulty of quantifying the benefits of R&D investment, SFAS No. 2 requires companies to treat the entire outlay as an expense. Consequently, Lucent's total assets and net income are effectively understated. Some of the market price for Lucent shares reflects technology advantages provided by its R&D. At the end of fiscal 1998, the market value of Lucent common stock was about $91 billion. Meanwhile, the book value of stockholders' equity was $5.5 billion. Every year Lucent expenses all its R&D investment. Every year, the difference between the market and book value of its stockholders' equity grows larger.

Similar distortions occur for other sorts of intangible assets. Expenditures to establish brand-name associations (e.g., Sony dependability, "Miller time", "Ford trucks are built tough") and other advertising costs are expensed. The reasoning is analogous to the treatment for R&D: benefits are difficult to measure reliably. Likewise, the know-how and expertise a company develops from manufacturing its products or delivering services does not appear as an asset on the balance sheet. "Human" capital is thus another intangible that GAAP ignores.

Some intangibles are capitalized and put on the balance sheet. The cost of establishing a patent, copyright, or trademark is treated as an asset. Note, however, that the cost of developing a patented item is R&D, and would be expensed. Exclusionary rights (e.g., a cable license, a cellular service territory, or a taxi medallion) are also intangibles. They are reported as assets, but valued at historical cost, despite the considerable market potential monopoly power offers.

Understanding how GAAP treats intangibles lets us appreciate the orientation of historical-cost financial statements. If a company invests in projects that have uncertain future benefits, the book value of its equity tends to understate market value. This phenomenon is particularly pronounced in industries that invest in large amounts of R&D. The reported earnings of pharmaceutical, biotechnology, and software firms are generally lower than they would be if their R&D costs were capitalized. Their assets are understated, as is their stockholders' equity, which in turn raises the observed rates of return on assets and return on equity.

KEY 14

You got the basics, so how are financial data used to compare one firm with another?

uppose you are considering an investment in Compaq Computer Corporation. Competitors in the computer industry include Dell, Gateway, and Apple. You may decide to ignore IBM and Hewlett-Packard, which also make personal computers, because they are in too many other businesses as well. They are not "pure plays."

After obtaining financial statements (see Key 25) from the different firms, the next step is to analyze them to learn about the operations and performance. Cross-sectional analysis is the basic approach used to assess a company in comparison with its competitors.

First, identify the important drivers of stock-price appreciation in the industry. Sales growth—the percentage change in sales from one period to another—is probably the most important. If the financial reports break down revenue by segments like hardware, software, and services, you can

> A banker is a fellow
> who lends his umbrella
> when the sun is shining
> and wants it back the
> minute it begins to rain.

Mark Twain

compare the relative proportions among the competitors. Or you can use the footnotes to evaluate which firms will reap greater benefits from foreign investments, if you suspect their overseas markets are growing faster than the domestic market (see Keys 23 and 24).

Profitability is also an important factor. To evaluate it, prepare common-size statements by dividing each income statement line by revenue. Each item is thus expressed as a percentage of Revenue. Common-size statements permit comparisons between different-sized firms. Earnings as a percentage of sales is a common profitability measure.

Other income statement data are critical. The Gross Margin ratio (Revenue less Cost of Goods Sold, divided by Revenue), and Selling, General and Administrative Expenses (as a percentage of revenue) provide further information as to why profitability differs among companies. Your review could prompt further investigation.

Suppose you learn from your examination that Dell's business model has a lower cost structure than its rivals do? If you estimate the proportion of costs that are fixed and variable you'll have insight into how earnings will change if a firm experiences a jump in its revenue.

The duPont formula is an oft-used tool for analysis. Its virtue is linking profitability from the income statement to the investment base on the balance sheet. The formula is:

$$(\text{Earnings/Sales}) \times (\text{Sales/Average total assets}) = (\text{Earnings/Average total assets})$$

Profitability (Earnings/Sales) is multiplied by Turnover (Sales/Assets). The result is a measure of how much profit is earned on the asset base. One company may generate more revenue per dollar of investment. This could occur because of greater manufacturing productivity, extensive outsourcing, leased rather than purchased equipment, or tighter control of inventory. If two firms' profitability ratios are the same, than the company with higher turnover will have a larger return on its asset base. The duPont approach captures these effects.

If a company is able to earn a higher return on assets than its borrowing cost (i.e., its after-tax cost of debt), its stockholders will enjoy this extra margin. The differential return increases return on equity (net income less preferred dividends, divided by average stockholders' equity).

This is the result of leverage, the strategy of borrowing funds at x%, and employing them for the benefit of stockholders so they earn (x+y)%. Leverage can be measured several ways. Perhaps the most common approach is by dividing average total assets (total assets at year's beginning and end, divided by two) by average common stockholders' equity. A second measure, the debt-equity ratio divides long term debt by stockholder's equity. A third measure models leverage as long-term debt divided by total capitalization (long term debt plus equity).

Industries with relatively stable revenues and expenses are able to carry higher levels of debt. For example, financial service companies typically are highly leveraged. Because profit margins are narrow in this industry, the use of leverage is crucial to increasing stockholders' return. Managers use the liquidity and relative stability of cash flows from financial services to enable their greater use of debt.

You've just been introduced to cross-sectional analysis, profitability measures, and leverage. In Key 15, we'll discuss some additional techniques for analyzing financial statements.

KEY 15

Staying alive: analyzing financial data to measure the health and survivability of a firm

T ime-series analysis is another important tool for evaluating firms. In time-series approaches, data from one company are studied over a number of periods. To make sense of time-series data, corresponding time periods must be compared, because many industries experience wide variations in performance from one season to another.

This phenomenon is called seasonality. In retailing, for example, a large portion of the year's business is done in November and December. A comparison between the fourth and first quarter for a department store is not meaningful without adjusting for seasonality.

The first quarter is expected to have lower revenues and perhaps lower margins because of clearance sales. In contrast, the fourth quarter has higher labor costs from the increased staffing needed for longer holiday hours. For these reasons, an analyst will compare the current period with the corresponding period a year earlier and perhaps for several years before that. (GAAP requires firms to disclose operating results by quarter for at least the prior two years.)

Another year to year comparison that is important for retailers is same-store sales. Analysts need to investigate components of increased revenue. Part of the increase may be from adding new stores. But the bulk of the change is probably due to growth in sales at pre-existing stores. Time-series examination permits separation of these two effects. Time-series methods are often used to analyze data over a number of periods to isolate important trends.

Liquidity analysis is also critical to understanding the survivability of a firm and in determining its value in the event of financial distress (see Key 16). It is particularly important to creditors and, to a lesser extent, stockholders. If a company experiences problems repaying its debt, creditors will look to the debtor's assets. Perhaps the bulk of asset value is tied up in plant, property, and equipment. These may be highly specialized properties, and difficult to sell. In any event, a sale could take some time, even if the property were offered at a distress price. The assets are thus illiquid.

In contrast, a firm's marketable securities can be sold quickly to raise cash, generally at current market price levels. The securities are said to be liquid. In their ability to generate ready cash, most assets fall somewhere between the two extremes.

From the shareholder's standpoint, adequate liquidity allows a firm to cope with unanticipated situations. Favorable opportunities might require extra cash to invest in a marketing campaign or to finance the demands of a sharp increase in sales.

Adverse conditions tend to consume cash, so that liquid resources buy the company's executives time to respond. Further, many large companies seek to maintain their level of dividends to shareholders, regardless of temporary downturns. Sufficient liquidity, or ready access to borrowed funds, provides the means to continue such a policy.

Two measures of liquidity are working capital and the current ratio. Subtracting current liabilities from current assets yields working capital (CA − CL). This indicates liquidity by measuring cash on hand and cash generated by accounts receivable and inventory turnover that could be used to satisfy current liabilities.

The current ratio, derived by dividing current assets by current liabilities (CA / CL), is a second measure of liquidity. The current ratio can be modified into the quick or acid-test ratio. The quick ratio includes only those current assets that can be sold quickly. Typically, inventory and prepaid expenses are excluded (although some inventories such as precious metals or commodities have a ready market and may be included), and the remaining amount of current assets is divided by current liabilities.

These are just some of the tools useful for assessing financial statements. They all are helpful in using financial data to analyze a firm's current position and future prospects.

KEY 16

How great are the costs of financial distress?

Financial distress occurs if a firm is unable to meet obligations to lenders and creditors. Lenders and creditors suffer if they are not repaid in full; the distressed firm's stockholders suffer as well. There are various categories of financial distress. An academic study I co-authored is useful in understanding how to measure its costs for stockholders.

In "Interrelation among Events of Default" (*Contemporary Accounting Research*, fall 1995), Beneish and Press divide distress into three stages: Technical default, debt-service default, and bankruptcy.

Technical default occurs if a provision of a loan agreement is violated. The provisions, called covenants, specify actions a firm will undertake or refrain from. For example, a firm may promise that the total of its Cash, Marketable Securities, and Accounts Receivable will continue to exceed Accounts Payable by $5 million. Another company may pledge that the ratio of its Total Assets to Long-term Notes Payable will be greater than 2.75:1. Compliance with covenants is accomplished by monitoring financial results. Failure to be in compliance is technical default.

In a technical default, the deterioration of a firm's cash flow is not severe enough to preclude making promised interest or principal payments to lenders. When a company is unable to meet its contractual cash-flow obligations, it commits a debt-service default. Typically, such defaults lead to re-negotiation of the lending agreement. The defaulter faces increased borrowing cost, and makes concessions that limit managerial control.

In bankruptcy, a firm seeks protection from its creditors. Operational control is wrested from management, and assigned to a court-appointed trustee and a committee comprised of creditors. Chapter 11 of the Federal Bankruptcy Act describes the procedures under which a firm proposes a plan either to reorganize its activities, or to liquidate its assets and pay the proceeds to creditors and debtholders. It is common in both reorganization and liquidation for the stockholders' equity claim to end up worthless.

Daniel Beneish and I studied 159 incidents of distress that occurred between 1983 and 1987 among firms traded on the New York or American Stock Exchanges, or NASDAQ. We found profound economic effects of financial distress.

Bankruptcy filings have the most adverse impact on a firm's stock price. After adjusting for the overall behavior of the stock market during our investigation period, we found that bankrupt firms' stock prices decreased by an average of 30 percent in the three-day period centered on the announcement of bankruptcy. (Returns measured after adjusting for overall stock market conditions are called abnormal returns. Announcements include stories in the *Wall Street Journal, Dow Jones News Service*, or items reported in a firm's Form 10-K filings.) Beneish and I estimate that stockholders of the average bankrupt firm can expect to lose $20 million from the effect of the announcement itself.

This loss is on top of an average 62 percent loss that occurs during the 15 months preceding the bankruptcy announcement. Even before a bankruptcy filing, the public usually learns about the dire financial straits of most firms that ultimately file Chapter 11.

Stockholders of firms that default on debt service also suffer large losses. The average abnormal loss in the three-day period around news of a debt-service default is 11 percent, which translates into a $7 million loss. The abnormal loss during the 15 months prior to the news is 39 percent.

Unsurprisingly, stockholders in firms announcing technical defaults suffer smaller losses. The average effect of the announcement of a technical default is an abnormal loss of 3.5 percent, equivalent to a loss of $2.5 million. In the 15 months prior to news of a technical default, the average share for a technical defaulter lost 19 percent compared with the overall market.

The study is unique in examining the continuum of default events. Other academic papers that assess the categories of distress separately corroborate these results. Financial distress has disastrous effects on stock prices. The techniques for assessing profitability and liquidity in Keys 12, 14, and 15 are tools for identifying potentially troubled firms.

KEY 17

Estimating the cost of using up productive capacity: depreciation

D epreciation is the allocation of the cost of a fixed asset over the years of its use. Fixed assets (also called long-lived assets) represent the capital investments that provide a firm with its means to produce goods or deliver services. Each year, the expense for using the fixed assets is included in the income statement as Depreciation Expense.

Accountants consider most fixed assets to have limited useful lives. (Land is considered to have an unlimited useful life and is not depreciated.) The estimated useful lives of the fixed assets and the methods used to calculate depreciation are discussed in the footnotes to the financial statements. Fixed assets are generally reported in the balance sheet at net book value—historical cost less accumulated depreciation. An asset's accumulated depreciation is the sum of all depreciation expense recorded since its acquisition.

There are a variety of methods used to calculate

depreciation. The calculation involves estimating the useful life of the asset and choosing a depreciation method. Depreciation approaches include the straight-line, accelerated, and units-of-production methods.

For example, Threadbare Company expects to use a milling machine for five years. Under the straight-line method, the asset's cost is allocated equally to each year of its useful life. The annual depreciation expense would be 20 percent of the machine's depreciable cost (original cost less estimated salvage value).

Under accelerated methods, more depreciation is recorded in the early years of an asset's life compared with its later years. Using the double-declining balance (DDB) method for the milling machine (one of several accelerated approaches), depreciation is calculated for the first year as 40 percent of the machine's cost less accumulated depreciation. The following year, the remaining balance is depreciated by 40 percent, and so on for the estimated life of the machine, until the book value of the machine reaches the salvage estimate. Note the DDB rate is double the straight-line rate.

With the units-of-production method, the company needs an estimate of the total production output of the machine over its useful life. The annual depreciation charge is based on the machine's actual, annual output compared to the estimated output over its life. Under GAAP, companies are required to disclose, in the footnotes, the useful lives of fixed assets and the methods used to calculate depreciation.

Depreciation expense is added back to net income on the statement of cash flows to arrive at

Cash Provided by Operations. Depreciation expense reduces net income, but does not use cash. To adjust net income to get cash from operations, accountants add back non-cash expenses such as depreciation. The cash flows related to fixed assets occur only in the years assets are acquired or sold.

The estimates used in preparing financial statements are usually different from the methods used in calculating depreciation for a firm's corporate tax return. Federal and state tax laws govern the calculation of depreciation for tax purposes. These laws have a different objective than GAAP depreciation guidelines.

For example, the Federal government may encourage capital investment by allowing companies to depreciate their equipment over a shorter period. (The increased expense on the tax return reduces reported income, and thus tax liability. This makes investment more attractive.) Don't confuse the depreciation expense reported on a company's financial statements with the amounts used in reporting tax liability to the government.

KEY 18

Computing cost of goods sold, and valuing inventory

Cost of Goods Sold (COGS) is the largest expense on many company's income statements. What makes up COGS? In retailing, firms acquire finished goods to resell at a higher price. In manufacturing and the delivery of services, a firm uses its facilities to transform labor and materials into products or a service. On the income statement, the expense of buying or making products sold is labeled Cost of Goods Sold, and is matched against Sales revenue. The difference between Sales and COGS is known as Gross Profit (or, Gross Margin).

To compute COGS, firms use either a perpetual or periodic inventory costing system. A running balance of COGS is maintained under a perpetual system. Each time a product is sold, COGS is increased and inventory is decreased by the cost of the product.

Under a periodic system, which computes COGS only once per accounting period, COGS is calculated according to the following procedure:

$$\text{Beginning inventory} + \text{Purchases} =$$
$$\text{Cost of goods available for sale}$$

$$\text{Cost of goods available for sale} - \text{Ending inventory} =$$
$$\text{Cost of goods sold}$$

Beginning Inventory is the cost of inventory on last year's balance sheet. Ending Inventory is the cost of products on hand at the end of the period, computed as the sum of the number of units times their costs. Businesses take counts of inventory as close as possible to the end of the period. An accounting period can be a month, quarter, or year in duration.

Consider the unit costs used to value inventory. Which unit costs are used if a company has purchased an item at various prices during the period? For example, Newco Racquets purchased 10 squash racquets for $50 each during its first month of operations (it had no Beginning Inventory). Later in the quarter, the firm purchased five more racquets at $62 each. In total, it sold 10 racquets during its first three months. There are several approaches to assigning costs to Ending Inventory and COGS.

Date	Transaction	Cost
Oct. 4	Purchased 10 racquets	$500
Dec. 5	Purchased 5 racquets	$310

The first-in, first-out (FIFO) method assigns unit costs from the earliest purchases to COGS. Costs from the latest purchases are used for Ending Inventory. Using FIFO, Newco Racquets reports COGS of $500 (the 10 racquets at $50). Ending Inventory is valued at $310 (the later purchase of five racquets, at $62 each).

Under last-in, first-out (LIFO), different results obtain. The LIFO method assigns unit costs from the latest purchases to COGS. Costs from the earliest purchases are used for Ending Inventory. Under LIFO, Newco reports COGS of $560 (its most recent purchases of racquets, five at $62 and five at $50). Ending Inventory is valued at $250 (the earliest purchases of five racquets, at $50 each).

Under the weighted-average cost method, the average unit cost of Beginning Inventory and purchases is computed. Average cost is the sum of (Beginning Inventory and Purchases), divided by the number of units. The average unit cost is used to value both Ending Inventory and COGS. For Newco, the average unit cost is $54 ($810 of purchases divided by 15 units). COGS would be $540 ($54 times 10) and Ending Inventory, $270 ($54 times five units).

When unit costs are changing different methods lead to different COGS and Ending Inventory amounts. When unit costs are rising, LIFO will generate the highest COGS because the method uses the most recent purchases. When unit costs are decreasing, FIFO will result in the highest COGS because it uses the oldest purchases.

If prices are rising it is advantageous for firms to use LIFO for preparing their tax return because it provides the highest COGS, which in turn leads to a lower taxable income. Under Federal tax law, companies that use LIFO for their tax return must also use it for financial reporting. To save on income taxes, such companies also end up reporting higher COGS, which translates into lower net income on their financial statements than if they used FIFO.

GAAP requires LIFO-basis companies to disclose in their footnotes the difference between LIFO and current cost values of their inventory. By adding this amount (known as the LIFO reserve) to inventory, the value of inventory on a FIFO basis can be approximated. Thus, the change in the LIFO reserve from last year gives us the difference between LIFO and FIFO COGS. If the LIFO reserve increased by $100,000 during a year, then COGS would be $100,000 lower than if the firm had used FIFO. By adjusting for LIFO reserve amounts, you can compare the operating results of LIFO and FIFO firms. This is an important tool when making cross-sectional comparisons (see Key 14).

What good, honest,

generous men at home

will be wolves and foxes

on change!

Emerson, Conduct of Life

KEY 19

What do we have to pay?
Accounting for taxes

onsistent with the matching principle, income tax expense is reported in the same year as the revenues and expenses that generate it. Under GAAP, tax expense is calculated as a percentage of (revenue less expenses). Income tax expense, however, is not necessarily the same as the amount of taxes the corporation actually pays for the year. How does that happen? In any year, revenues and expenses for financial reporting and for tax purposes are likely to differ.

There are two causes for the divergence: permanent differences, and timing differences. Permanent differences are revenue or expense items that will never be included on the tax return because of tax code proscriptions. Tax-exempt municipal bond interest (a revenue item) and non-deductible officers' life-insurance premiums (an expense item) are examples. Neither will ever appear on a tax return, yet both appear on the income statement.

Recognizing revenue or expense items on the financial statements in different years from the tax return causes timing differences. A firm may recognize revenue upon sale for the financial statements, but for the tax return, by using the installment method, revenue is not recognized until cash is collected.

Why bother doing this? From the perspective of financial reporting, it may be advantageous to recognize revenue as soon as possible. But paying taxes uses cash. So, from a tax perspective, it is best to find a method that defers recognizing revenue—thus delaying cash outlays for taxes.

Using different depreciation methods for the financial statements and tax return will also create a timing difference. Unlike a permanent difference, a timing difference item will eventually show up on both places. The issue is when.

Deferred taxes are the tax effects of timing differences between the amounts of assets and liabilities for financial reporting purposes and the amounts used for income tax purposes (per SFAS No.109). The income tax liability a corporation owes for a given year is based on taxable income. Income tax expense is based on financial statement Net Income (after adjusting for permanent differences). The difference between these amounts is the current-year adjustment to deferred taxes.

A deferred tax liability occurs when a company deducts expenses on the tax return prior to reporting them on the income statement, or when it includes revenue on the income statement prior to including it on the tax return. For example, a deferred tax liability results from using accelerated depreciation for the tax return and straight-line depreciation for the income statement. The carrying amount or book value of fixed assets will be different for financial reporting and tax purposes.

A deferred tax asset results when a firm reports expenses on the income statement prior to deducting them on the tax return, or when it includes revenue on the tax return prior to recognizing it in the income statement. A warranty arrangement is a good example. A manufacturer includes Warranty Revenue on its tax return upon sale of an item and a warranty contract. For the financial statements, matching requires the manufacturer recognize Warranty Revenue over the warranty's life. The effect is that the tax return gets ahead of the income statement in recognizing revenue; this generates a deferred tax asset.

Under GAAP, a corporation must break down its tax expense by the tax owed for the current year and the adjustment to deferred taxes. In addition, the firm discloses the significant sources of deferred tax items. Corporations must also provide a reconciliation between their effective tax rate (their income tax expense divided by net income before taxes) and the federal tax rate (as of 1999) of 35 percent. State and foreign taxation items and permanent effects typically explain any differences.

KEY 20

Don't overlook long-term obligations: debt and leases

A firm raises capital in two ways: by selling stock, or issuing debt. Keys 9 and 3 discussed the issuing of stock. What are some reasons management might choose to issue debt?

First, because debt ownership confers no right to vote on corporate matters, issuing debt preserves each stockholder's proportionate claim and say in corporate affairs. Second, debt has tax advantages. The interest paid on debt is a deduction for Federal income tax purposes; dividends (the return paid to stockholders) are not deductible. The deductibility of interest expense is, in effect, a Government subsidy that favors debt instruments over equity. Third, debt may be the only means to raise capital. While there are exceptions (witness the hot market for Internet initial public offerings) many firms are too small to have a ready market for their equity. The only means to raise capital might be through taking out loans or issuing notes payable. Fourth, management's profit-making strategy might include leverage. Recall from Key

The buck stops with the guy
who signs the checks.

Rupert Murdoch

14 that the idea of leverage is to sell debt at rate x%, and then to invest in projects that earn (x+y)%. Use of leverage is a way to boost the returns enjoyed by stockholders.

Debt and leases are major long-term obligations. Long-term liabilities, according to Key 3, will not require satisfaction during the next year. Long-term debt items, including bonds, debentures, and notes payable, possess common characteristics. Typically, the buyer of a debt issue receives a two-part promise. The first part is a promise from the issuer to redeem (buy back) the instrument at its face value (called par value) at maturity. Second, the firm promises to make fixed, periodic interest payments to the owner until redemption.

Let's consider an example. Melea Dee, Incorporated needs capital to build a new factory in Donut Plaines, Indiana. It plans to issue

$90,000,000 of 15 year, 7.25% notes on December 1, 1999. The notes pay interest semi-annually.

Melea Dee is offering 90,000 notes in the market, in $1,000 denominations. ($1,000 is the customary amount for the face value on a bond or note.) On December 1, 2014, the firm promises to buy back all its notes for $1,000 each. During the interim, Melea Dee will pay $36.25 per note to each owner of record every six months. (Bonds and notes customarily pay interest every six months. Thus, each owner each year receives [7.25% / 2] × $1000 × 2 = $72.50 per bond.)

Debt owners are often protected by covenants—promises by the issuing firm to take certain actions, and to refrain from others. Penalties are provided for violating covenants, which reduces the risk of holding debt by constraining the behavior of the issuer.

A lease is an arrangement in which the lessor (owner) grants the lessee (user of the property) the right to use property for a period of time. The property can be land, a machine, a building, or some other depreciable asset. Leasing is used extensively in the transportation industry, by retailers, and in numerous settings where lessees can exploit its advantages. What are they?

First, there is a contractual advantage. Unlike a debt agreement that may contain covenants, leases tend to have fewer restrictions. While it is common to see many company assets pledged as collateral in debt agreements, the lessor's claim generally is secured only by the leased property.

Second, a lease can offer tax advantages. Lease payments are often fully deductible expenses, for tax purposes. Even if the actual useful life of the asset (see Key 17) exceeds the lease duration, the lessee can deduct the payments as expenses, which accelerates expense recognition.

Third, there is a potential financial reporting advantage. If a lease is structured to qualify for operating lease treatment, neither the asset nor the long-term liability shows up on the balance sheet. This raises the observed rate of return on assets and reduces leverage, since liabilities are lower. The benefits of better returns and lower leverage can translate into a lower cost of capital for the firm.

We saw in Key 9 that the Statement of Changes in Stockholders' Equity reports the details of transactions related to the company's activities in selling or buying back its stock. There is no equivalent statement, however, that reports transactions affecting debt. So how can an investor learn about activity involving debt and leases?

The footnotes are the place to look. The debt footnote breaks down a firm's long-term obligations by specific issue, gives the maturity dates, and the amounts outstanding. Many firms report whether they are in compliance with the covenants in their debt agreements, and some mention the explicit constraints they face. The footnote contains a schedule of future redemption payments.

The lease footnote explains the firm's activities, both as lessor and lessee. Firms provide a schedule of their minimum required future payments under non-cancelable operating leases. The obligations to satisfy debt claims and lease obligations can create potentially significant demands on cash. This is important information for understanding future cash flows.

KEY 21

More long-term obligations: pensions and other benefits

Corporations frequently provide retirement benefits, such as pension or health coverage, to their employees. The corporation can promise to provide certain benefits following an employee's retirement, known as a defined benefit plan, or to contribute to an investment account for the employee's retirement benefits, called a defined contribution plan.

To illustrate the difference, consider a defined benefit plan that promises to pay an employee $1,000 annually during retirement for each year of her tenure with the firm. By contrast, a defined contribution plan would promise to pay $1,000 annually to the employee's retirement account while she is working.

For both types of plans, corporations pay into a trust, an entity separate from itself, which invests the funds and pays benefits. The corporation's liability, however, is different under the two arrangements. In a defined contribution plan, the corporation has no continuing liability once the contributions are paid. In a defined benefit plan, the corporation is responsible for the promised benefits even if there are insufficient trust assets to cover them.

GAAP describes two types of defined benefit arrangements, pension- and post-retirement benefit (PRB) plans. Pensions provide monthly income, while PRB plans provide other benefits such as health coverage and life insurance.

A plan's obligations (the present value of the future benefits) and its assets can be substantial. For example, Lucent Technologies discloses a pension obligation of $27.8 billion and a PRB obligation of $9.2 billion in its 1998 annual report. Its plan assets are $36.2 billion and $4.0 billion respectively. Note that the pension plan's assets are more than Lucent's total assets on the balance sheet of $26.7 billion! In fact, when plan assets are this large, their investment performance can have a significant impact on a corporation's profitability.

How does the investment performance of the assets held in the plan affect company profitability? GAAP pension rules require companies to include any over- (under-) funding of the pension plan as an asset (or liability) on the balance sheet. (A plan is over-funded if its assets are greater than its obligations.) Assuming a plan is already fully funded, if its investments perform well—as most have in the long stock market boom of the past two decades—over-funding will increase. This change reduces the pension cost reported in the income statement.

Lucent's pension plan is over-funded. Thus the company includes an asset of $3.7 billion on the balance sheet that reflects this fact. Typically with a pension plan, we would expect an expense on the income statement. Lucent's pension experience actually increased its net income during each of the last three years. Performance of the pension plan's assets was so good that investment income exceeded the additional benefits earned by employees and more than met the assumed return built into the plan.

In the past, many companies recorded expense for post-retirement benefits as they spent cash, but did not record a liability for future benefits. The new rules for such plans require companies to record an expense and a liability over an employee's career for promised future benefits. In changing to the new rules implemented by SFAS No.106, many firms immediately had to record a liability for future post-retirement benefits that employees had earned based on their past service. These sums reached into the hundreds of billions of dollars for American corporations as a whole. Firms were also offered the choice of "catching up" by gradually recording the liability over a number of years.

This adjustment substantially increased liabilities and reduced shareholders' equity for a number of companies. Lucent's liability in excess of its plan assets is $5.1 billion. This represents almost a quarter of its total liabilities, and is nearly as large as stockholders' equity. Clearly, pensions and other benefits are a significant item in the financial statements.

KEY 22

Untangling the web of inter-corporate investments

U nder GAAP, there are three approaches to reporting the ongoing effects of one company's investment in another firm: the consolidation, equity, and cost methods. We will discuss these in terms of a parent company and a subsidiary it owns.

How the parent reports its investment depends on the level of its control over the subsidiary. Consolidated statements should be presented if the parent company owns more than half of the subsidiary's stock. The equity method is used when the parent owns between 20 percent and 50 percent. For passive investments (under 20 percent ownership), the cost method is used.

In a consolidated statement, the firms are presented as if they were a single legal entity. The financial statements for the parent and subsidiary are combined and any transactions between them (known as "intra-company transactions") are eliminated. Thus, for example, the consolidated cash balance adds the cash of both together, and accounts receivable is comprised of the parent's accounts plus its subsidiaries' accounts, less any amounts owed from one to the other. Similarly, for reported Revenue, after totaling the two, subtract any sales between parent and subsidiary.

The equity method can be thought of as a "one-line consolidation". The parent's investment in its subsidiary is shown on one line as an asset on the balance sheet. The parent's share of the subsidiary's net income (based on its ownership percentage) is reported on one line of its income statement. The remaining balance sheet and income statement amounts reflect the parent alone. The investment amount shown on the parent's balance sheet increases by its share of its subsidiary's net income, and decreases to reflect dividends received from the unit. Net income for the parent using the equity method is the same as consolidated net income for the parent and subsidiary together.

It is common for firms to invest excess cash in other companies' common stocks. Under the cost method, these passive investments (ownership interest less than 20 percent) are reported at market value on the balance sheet if they are liquid and can be easily converted to cash. Dividends appear on the income statement. Changes in value also appear on the income statement if the investments are "bought and held principally for the purpose of selling them in the near term" (per SFAS No.115). Otherwise, changes in value are reported in a separate component of stockholders' equity (see Key 9). Non-marketable investments are reported at the lower of cost or market value on the balance sheet.

Now consider the two methods for recording the

acquisition of a company: purchase, and pooling-of-interests. When the purchase method is used, buying another company is viewed as similar to buying any other asset. The acquired company is initially recorded at the price paid for it. This price needs to be allocated to the individual assets of the new subsidiary.

The acquired subsidiary's assets and liabilities are revalued to their estimated value on the purchase date. Any excess of the purchase price over the total value of the assets minus liabilities is called goodwill, an intangible asset. The consolidated income statement includes revenues and expenses of the subsidiary following the purchase date. Depreciation and amortization expense for the subsidiary is based on its revalued assets. (Amortization is the depreciation of intangible assets such as Patents and Goodwill.)

By contrast, the pooling-of-interests method takes the position that the two firms in a merger have not really changed. What occurs is a combination of ownership interests. Under this method, the assets and liabilities of the newly acquired subsidiary are not revalued as of the merger date. Instead, the consolidated balance sheet and income statement for the parent and subsidiary are prepared as if these firms had always been merged.

The purchase and pooling methods can produce very different results. If the pooling method is used for a merger occurring on the last day of the year, the income statement will include revenues and expenses for both firms for the entire year.

Under the purchase method, however, the income statement includes only one day of revenues and expenses for the acquired firm! Because the assets are revalued and goodwill is recorded, depreciation and amortization expense after the acquisition will be higher using the purchase method.

Most companies prefer to use the pooling-of-interests method for acquisitions because it allows them to report a higher net income. In April 1999, however, the FASB threatened this popular method by voting unanimously to eliminate pooling. FASB Chairman Edmund Jenkins noted, "The Board decided it is hard for investors to make sound decisions about combining companies when two different accounting treatments exist for what is essentially the same transaction." As of spring 1999, the plan is to eliminate pooling-of-interest accounting by late 2000.

If you owe your bank a hundred pounds, you have a problem; but... if you owe your bank a million, it has.

John Maynard Keynes,
Down Communism's Sink

KEY 23

Is my company global? Should I care?

D id the high-profile mergers of Ford with Volvo, Daimler-Benz with Chrysler, and Universal Studios with Polygram catch your attention? It's clear that companies are expanding operations worldwide. Even if you don't own shares in Daimler-Benz, British Telecom, or Sony, as an investor you're probably already realizing returns from the global economy, while bearing its risks. How? Most large firms incorporated in the United States have major operations around the world, and the number is rapidly expanding.

Cola-Cola, for example, generates over 63 percent of its $19 billion of sales outside North America; over 60 percent of its net income comes from non-U.S. operations. In fact, the average firm in the S&P 500 realizes about 40 percent of its revenue overseas, according to Prudential Securities.

To determine the extent of a firm's multinational

activities, you should turn to data disclosed in financial statement footnotes. SFAS No.131 is part of an international effort to harmonize accounting policies regarding activities outside a company's home base. The new standard requires any American corporation with more than 10 percent of its revenues or assets outside of the United States to report the non-domestic revenue and assets separately, and provide at least one income measure broken down geographically. Firms can choose operating income (about 60 percent do so), or net income before or after taxes, by operational region(s).

Under SFAS No.131, each firm defines its own operational regions. One consequence of this freedom is some difficulty in comparing geographic segments across firms. An analyst might want to know, for example, which telecommunications company is most profitable in Europe. Good luck. A firm has full latitude to decide which countries are in its "Europe" region, as well as in defining what comprises segment income.

There is another difficulty in using segment data. The FASB does not require the consolidated basis for segment data presentation. Thus, the sum of sales by each segment could exceed the total sales for the firm. How? Sales made by one unit in a vertically integrated corporation to another unit of the same firm (a "family member") would be double counted if they were not eliminated.

Do global operations matter? An academic study by Bodnar and Weintrop (*Journal of Accounting & Economics*, 1997) finds that a dollar earned overseas has a significantly higher impact in establishing stock prices in U.S. markets than a dollar of income generated from domestic operations. The premium arises from the higher growth in

return on investment earned by foreign subsidiaries. Other academic studies show the value
of American firms increases when they expand
their overseas operations, in comparison to similar domestic firms that do not expand their foreign operations.

When companies based in the United States go
overseas, stockholders earn the rewards but still
enjoy the SEC's disclosure requirements.
American management reports the results of operations, while a global auditing firm attests to the
reliability of the company's statements.

KEY 24

What am I buying if I purchase a foreign firm's stock?

Familiar names such as Sony, Nokia, and Unilever are among the 1,415 depository receipt companies that were listed on U.S. stock exchanges in 1998. More than 500 foreign companies trade on the New York Stock Exchange as depositary receipts, accounting for $440 billion of trading volume in 1998.

A prospective international investor needs to understand two important features about purchasing foreign securities.

First, an investor in the United States *does not* actually purchase shares in the foreign firm. Rather, the investor purchases a negotiable certificate known as a depositary receipt, that represents a company's publicly traded equity or debt. There are two types of receipts, American (ADR), or Global (GDR).

Depositary receipts are created when a broker purchases and holds a foreign company's shares

There are two times in a man's life when he should not speculate: when he can't afford it, and when he can.

Mark Twain, Following the Equator,
Pudd'nhead Wilson's New Calendar

on its home-country stock market. The depositary receipts then can trade freely, just like any other security on a stock or bond exchange, and are priced and pay dividends in U.S. dollars.

The Bank of New York (www.bankofny.com) is a large broker of ADRs and GDRs. It buys securities on foreign exchanges, and then offers ADRs in the United States. Its web site contains a wealth of information about the market. If you'd like to obtain detailed financial information on a wide variety of ADRs, a J.P. Morgan web site (www.adr.com) is worth studying.

The second feature in investing abroad is the challenge of evaluating foreign firms. Foreign companies traded on the NYSE file a Form 20-F, which is the similar to a Form 10-K filing. The 20-F filer provides a balance sheet and income statement prepared according to the accounting principles of the firm's host county, with values denominated in the local currency. But in return for the privilege of access to U.S. capital markets, the SEC requires a Form 20-F filer to reconcile its net income and retained earnings. This is done by comparing the amounts obtained under the foreign accounting policy with the figures from following Generally Accepted Accounting Principles in the United States. The reconciliation appears as a footnote in the 20-F.

The major differences in accounting policies between U.S. GAAP and the rest of the world tend to be in accounting for pensions, research and development, and consolidations. Many firms outside the United States do not fully match pension costs with current income (see Key 21). What's more, firms capitalize their research and development cost in most countries. (Recall from Key 13 that U.S. GAAP requires R&D costs to be written off in the year they are incurred.)

A second difference is that the U.S.-style pooling of interests is infrequently used in international settings (see Key 22). Almost all non-U.S. multinational conglomerates use the purchase method of consolidation. Further, most international companies write off reported goodwill from purchase acquisitions in a very short period of time. U.S. GAAP permits goodwill to be amortized over a period of up to 40 years, although current FASB deliberations contemplate shortening the period.

Are differences in accounting policy likely to decrease as the world's economies come closer together? The International Accounting Standards

Committee (IASC) is the body that writes IAS, the International Accounting Standards adopted in global markets. Although the IASC has no formal regulatory power, its members represent over 100 professional agencies from 75 countries. The goal of the IASC is to work toward worldwide harmonization of accounting standards, regulations, and procedures for the presentation of financial statements.

Jeffery Garten, Dean of the Yale School of Management, suggested in a recent article (*Business Week*, April 5, 1999) that harmonization of international standards is at least a decade away. He notes that accounting-standard setters in the United States believe that our reporting system is the best in the world, and they seem unwilling to move U.S. GAAP toward international congruence. Don't expect any significant relaxation of U.S. disclosure rules in the near future.

One way to understand the differences in financial statement presentation is to look at the results of a specific foreign company. Nokia (www.nokia.com), the Finnish telecommunications giant best known for its mobile phones, does a good job in making its financial information available on the Web. The Investors' section of its site includes the company's quarterly press releases and conference calls. The footnotes in Nokia's 1998 annual report explain how the use of GAAP instead of IAS would affect its financial statements. The notes explain the factors that cause these differences—an example of the reconciliation required by Form 20-F.

KEY 25

What are other sources of financial information?

O.K., you have just read 24 keys about how to understand and use the basic financial statements. What if you want to know more? Plenty of other resources are available to you on the Web, in print and in other forms that are useful for collecting and evaluating financial information.

Annual statements, footnotes, and Management Discussions typically appear in Forms 10-K. Since January 1994 these reside online at EDGAR (Electronic Data Gathering Analysis and Retrieval) on the SEC site (www.sec.gov/edaux). Forms 10-Q, 8-K, registration statements, and other filings are also available there as free downloads. The time series of EDGAR data only runs about four years. Disclosure, Inc. (www.disclosure.com) sells SEC filings on microfiche, hardcopy, or compact disk. Its Worldscope product covers 15,000 companies involved in global operations. Many universities and public libraries maintain collections of

If genius means
extraordinary energy
allied to extraordinary
originality, the great
financier is undoubtedly
a genius.

Robertson Davies,
Moonbeams From The Larger Lunacy

Disclosure products, and are a good resource for archival research.

Information downloads from EDGAR tends to be unwieldy. Other services have risen to the need for spreadsheet-friendly data management. 10Kwizard (www.tenkwizard.com) lets you select sections of the Form 10-K to view and print. Another free source for filings is Freeedgar (www.freeedgar.com).

If you are only interested in annual reports, The Public Register's Annual Report Service (www.prars.com) makes them available at no cost. Most companies also will usually provide them through their Shareholder Relations office. The best way, in most cases, is to view them online or download the report from the company's web site.

Standard and Poor's (www.spglobal.com) compiles corporate data on tapes and compact disk, and offers the data in 20-year time series. The tape product is called Compustat, (www.compustat.com) and is widely used by financial analysts and academic researchers. It contains balance sheet, income statement, and cash flow data for firms on the New York and American Stock Exchange, as well as NASDAQ companies. S&P also offers a product that runs on desktop computers, Compustat PC. Its data and access program are sold on a compact disk. S&P's Global Vantage database covers 11,000 firms across 70 countries.

There are dozens of sites that offer stock quotes, charts, and news. *Market Guide Investor* (www.marketguide.com) provides free real-time quotes, financial data on 12,000 companies, earnings estimates, and commentary. Quote.com (www.quote.com) and CNNFn (www.cnnfn.com) stream prices and offer news and analysis. Business Week Online and Financenter (www.businessweek.com, and www.finan-center.com) provide charts, help investors make asset allocation decisions, and report news. The New York Times web site (www.nytimes.com) provides links to stock prices and financial information as well as in-depth business reporting. Hoover's Online (http://hoovers.com) offers free company capsules, financial statements, and IPO news.

Marketplayer (www.marketplayer.com) and Stock Selector (www.stockselector.com) provide users with analysis and stock charts, portfolio screens, and message service. Morningstar also offers a site (www.morningstar.com) that enables investors to run mutual funds and stocks through user specified screens. The Motley Fool (www.fool.com) offers an irreverent but informed perspective on investing, with extensive analysis and bulletin boards organized by ticker symbols. Its motto well-characterizes its style: "Educate, Amuse, Enrich".

There are hundreds of other offerings online. Search engines such as Excite (www.excite.com), InfoSeek (www.infoseek.com), or Ask Jeeves (www.askjeeves.com), which searches search engines, will tailor an inquiry to your precise needs.

The profound reduction in the cost of accessing data through the Internet levels the playing field for ordinary investors, and makes retrieval of financial information and exploration of investment opportunities easier than it has ever been. You can read analysts' earnings forecasts, study company profiles, or get the news. Who knows, now that you've learned some of the keys to analyzing financial statements, you may want to push your understanding further.

INDEX

AUTHOR

ERIC PRESS, Ph.D., is an Associate Professor of Accounting at the Fox School of Business and Management at Temple University, and is a CPA in Washington State. From 1994 to 1998, he was a member of the American Institute of Certified Public Accountant' SEC Regulations Committee. Dr. Press serves on editorial boards and as a referee at numerous publications, including *The Accounting Review*, *Contemporary Accounting Research*, *Accounting Horizons*, and *The Journal of Accounting and Public Policy*.

Acknowledgements
Special thanks go to Thomas Dowdell, CPA for his help with the project. Tom is my Research Assistant and a Ph.D. student in Accounting at Temple University. Joel Stiebel, CPA, and Professors Joe Weintrop of Baruch College and Daniel Beneish of Indiana University provided valuable comments on the manuscript.